THE GOD OF ALL GRACE

By Henry Newcome

COPYRIGHT INFORMATION

TABLE OF CONTENTS

MEET HENRY NEWCOME
by C. Matthew McMahon

Far before the Baptist Charles Spurgeon, Henry Newcome (1627-1695) was known as the Prince of Preachers. He was a native of Northhamptonshire, and educated at St. John's College in Cambridge where he earned a Master of Arts. After his conversion and resolve to follow Jesus Christ, his first position seems to have been in Goostree, and afterwards at Gosworth, in Cheshire. When Mr. Richard Hollingworth died, he received a unanimous invitation to assist Mr. Richard Heyrick at Manchester, a man of great esteem and worth. In replying to this call, Mr. Newcome was conflicted, having also received a call from Shrewsbury, and desired to ascertain the divine will in such a quandary. After much consideration and prayer he

accepted the position in Manchester in 1656, and continued there to his death.

In Manchester, throughout the course of his ministry, he found much use for his talents which were faithfully employed in his Christ's service. Not only did he labor within his own ministry, but he also took time to minister in the surrounding areas, and they too enjoyed the benefit of sitting under his preaching and teaching.

When King Charles took his throne, no longer in need of his Puritan friends, he was intolerant of them and produced the Act of Uniformity. The Puritans, including our Mr. Newcome, could not in good conscience and according to Scripture, comply with this act. Being forbid to preach, he relinquished his position and, instead, preached from his house. Along with others, Mr. Newcome was imprisoned and fined many times, as was the nature of the Puritans to do in obeying God rather than men. During some of his imprisonments, he wrote extensively which circulated throughout the country and were used for the up building of the saints. When the *Oxford Act* took place, and he was driven from the heart of his family and flock, he sojourned at Ellenbrook waiting an opportunity to return to his previous ministry.

After some indulgences were issued by King Charles, Mr. Newcome returned and preached to his congregation in a place deemed appropriate and lawful to do so. A chapel was built for him in what is now called Cross Street, but then an open field called Ackers. Here Mr. Newcome continued to administer the ordinances of the gospel with great acceptance and usefulness until September 20, 1695, on which day it pleased God to take him to his heavenly reward, at 68 years of age.

The loss to the church by Mr. Newcome was severely felt by the churches in his ministerial area, and Matthew Henry mentions it in his diary with more than common concern. His unusual gifts made him useful to Christ and gave him an eminent status, not only as a minister of the gospel, but as an instructor of youth, in both offices he was effective.

His published works are:

1. *The Sinner's hope*; a discourse on Ezra. 10.
2. *Usurpation defeated and David restored*; a Sermon on the restoration of Charles II.

3. *The Covenant of Grace effectually remembered, of the God of All Grace.*

4. *A Discourse on Psalm 105* with 1 Chron. 16:15.

5. *A Help to Duty in and Right Improvement of Sickness.*

6. *A Discourse on Job. 5:6-8.*

7. *A Treatise on Rash and Sinful Anger*, from Proverbs 25:28.

8. *A faithful Narrative of the Life and Death of that holy and laborious preacher Mr. John Machip*, late of Astbury, in Cheshire.

Mr. John Howe said of Mr. Newcome,

"It may be truly said of such a man, as unknown, and yet well known. They that knew him best, could know but a small part of his true and great worth; and might always apprehend when they knew most of him, there was still much more that they did not know. His most sincere and inartificial humility, still drawing a veil over his other excellencies, which it hid and adorned at once; so as the appetite of knowing more must always meet with a check, and an incitation at the same time. There was in him a large stock of solid learning and knowledge, always ready for use; for ostentation never. Conscience the most strict and steady to himself, and the remotest from censoriousness of other men. Eloquence without, any labor of his own, not imitable by the greatest labor of another. O! the strange way he had of insinuating and winding himself into his hearer's bosoms! I have sometimes heard him, when the only thing to be regretted was, that the sermon must so soon be at an end. Conversation, so facetious and instructive together, that they who enjoyed it, if they were capable of improving, it, could scarcely tell whether they went away from him more edified or delighted. *He was a burning and a shining light.* O! Manchester! Manchester! that ancient famed seat of religion and profession, may Capernaum's doom never be thine! May thy Heyrick, Hollingworth, Newcome, and thy neighbours Angier, and Harrison, and diverse more, never be witnesses against thee."

Mr. John Chorlton, who was his fellow laborer, and preached his funeral sermon, says of him,

> "He was a person of good natural parts, one that had enough of a genius to master what be applied himself to, and to make up the figure of a great man. These natural abilities were cultivated by extraordinary industry, which began very early and continued all his life; witness the many volumes he has left behind him written with his own hand. He was most conversant in those parts of learning which are directly subservient to divinity, and made great use thereof in all his composures; but with so little affectation, that the unlearned were never amused by it, and yet the judicious part of his auditory had no lack of it. His parts and learning were both admirably set off by a singular fitness for friendship and conversation, in which he was amiable above many. His temper was serene, candid, generous to, and beyond his power. His discourse was ingenuous, innocent, pleasant, and profitable to a high degree. His deportment was grave, yet

sweet and obliging. These virtues were lodged in a soul truly Christian. I know we must make some allowance for human infirmities, from which none are exempt while they are in the body. He was but a candidate for the state of perfection, and was a man subject to like passions as we are, which he had now put off together with mortality. But certainly, notwithstanding this, he had a truly Christian spirit, and did abound in choice experiences of God's dealing with himself and others. His life was filled up with a uniform series of faithful services to God and to his generation. He did not load men with heavy burdens, which, he would not touch with one of his fingers, but put his own neck into the same Christian yoke, which he exhorted others to take upon them. The greatest part of his character (his Christianity supposed,) is this, that he was an able and faithful minister of the Gospel, not of the letter, but of the Spirit. He was not only an excellent minister at large, but a prudent vigilant pastor to a numerous flock that dearly loved him, and was no less dearly beloved of him. How solicitous was he for the peace and holiness of his people! His preaching matter was solid and weighty, and of a practical tendency to change men's natures, and reform their lives. He was not for novel undigested speculations. He was a messenger, "and interpreter, one among a thousand, to show unto man his uprightness," (Job 33:23). His sermons were plain and discoursive and full of holy zeal and fervor...I do not present you with this account of this eminent and faithful servant of Christ, as if it were a full and perfect, character of him. No, that would require a larger compass, and an abler man than I can give it. This may suffice to be spoken at the present, to the honor of Divine grace, manifesting itself in so useful an instrument. May it also provoke us to bless God for him, and kindle in us an emulation of his attainments, and of the success that attended his labours," (stated in his funeral sermon by Mr. Chorlton for Mr. Newcome).

CHAPTER 1:
The Christian's God

"The God of all grace, who hath called us unto his eternal glory by Christ Jesus, after that ye have suffered awhile, make you perfect, stablish, strengthen, settle you," (1 Peter 5:10).

In these words we have a description of what God is in himself, he is *the God of all grace*; and what he has done for us, he, "hath called us unto eternal glory by Christ Jesus." From which you may observe, that it is the great comfort and advantage of a true Christian, in all his addresses to God, to look upon him and go unto him, as, "the God of all grace—and that it is the standing privilege of all true Christians, that God, "hath called them to his eternal glory by Christ Jesus."

We shall in this discourse speak a little to the first **DOCTRINE:** That it is the great comfort and advantage of a true Christian, in all his addresses to God, to look upon him and go to him as, "the God of all grace."

In prosecution of this doctrine we shall endeavor to show, first, how it is to be understood that

God is, "the God of all grace." Secondly, what advantage it is that we can look on God in this way. And then, thirdly, apply the subject.

First, how is it to be understood that God is, "the God of all grace?"

I. God may be said to be "the God of all grace" in the largest sense, take it which way you will.

1. He is the God of all grace *essentially*. He is, "the Lord, the Lord God, merciful and gracious, long-suffering, and abounding in goodness and truth." He is an infinitely gracious God; and it will appear so in *respect of his amiableness and beauty.*

All that loveliness that is in the creature is derived from God, and is but as a ray from that sun, a spark from that fire, and a drop from that fountain. "No man hath seen God at any time; the only begotten Son, which is in the bosom-of the Father, he hath declared him." And no man knows, "who the Father is, but the Son, and he to whom the Son will reveal him." The beauty of the blessed Deity was shown to us by Christ in the most familiar manner, for he is, "altogether lovely." There are several things which make men lovely. "A man's wisdom maketh his face to shine then God must be very lovely for he is, "the only wise God."

Condescension makes a man lovely; then how lovely was Christ who was, "meek and lowly of heart?" He never considered himself too great for any to approach who wished to come to him; he was familiar with lepers, with the sick, yes, with little children. Men are lovely when they are ready to do good on all occasions. Then, God is *very lovely*, for, "his tender mercies are over all his works," and he is good to the unthankful and unholy. Jesus Christ went about doing good, and God was manifest through the human nature of Christ. The glory of the Deity shone through him, and a spiritual knowledge of this amiableness of God attracts and delights the soul.

He is the, "God of all Grace," on account *of his clemency and condescension.*

One may have access to him with boldness through Christ, "Who is like unto the Lord our God, who dwelleth on high, who humbleth himself to behold the things that are in heaven, and in the earth," (Psa. 113:5-6). "What is man that thou art mindful of him?" It was condescension in God to look on man in his innocence, or to look on glorified spirits in heaven; but it is his pleasure to see his creatures happy, and he delights to do them good. It was grace in God that he made man happy at first, gave him such noble faculties, and entered into covenant with him; but his grace is manifested to us much more in our fallen condition now that we have forfeited all by sin, and made ourselves sinners, "God made man upright, but they have sought out many inventions." God might have left man in this state, but he is, "full of compassion."

It is infinite clemency in God that pardon should be enjoyed when a sinner repents. This is not after the manner of men. If a man accused before the judge were to say, all that has been sworn against me is true, and I have done *thus and thus*, but I am sorry for it, would it not be replied, what is that to us, we are sorry you took no better care, but the law must be observed? Man does not have power to forgive some offences; he is limited by God. Sometimes when a man has power in his hands to forgive another, he has no power in his heart. Not so with the God of all grace who has both authority and mercy, and when a sinner heartily repents through Jesus Christ he pardons and forgives him. This is infinite grace, and the convinced sinner thinks so when he feels the intolerable weight of sin removed, "Blessed is the man unto whom the Lord imputeth not iniquity, and in whose spirit there is no guile. When I kept silent my bones waxed old through my roaring all the day long. I said I will confess my transgressions unto the Lord; and thou forgavest the iniquity of my sin," (Psa. 32:2, 5).

It shows the infinite clemency of God to admit sinners into so near a relation, as that into which they are brought through Jesus Christ, "As many as received him, to them gave he power to become the sons of God, even to them that believe on his name," (John 1:12). If God were to pardon a poor wretch and let him live, it would be great grace, but much more that he should receive him into the number of his children. O! the infinite grace of God, that contrives everything to make those happy whom he loves; to make them his children! He gives them the disposition of children to love and fear him, and gives them a right to all the privileges of his children. This is the happiness of the regenerate.

He proves his clemency and condescension by hearing the prayers of his people. God is known by this character; a prayer hearing and answering God. His children, through Christ, prevail with him for what they need.

Is not this infinite grace, that he should listen to man; that it should be said, "This poor man cried and the Lord heard him?" God delights in the prayers of poor sinful creatures; and there is scarcely any great thing done for his church and people, but it comes in answer to prayer. He does not stir up his people to earnest prayer, but he hears them in what they pray for, "The effectual fervent prayer of a righteous man availeth much," (James 5:16). If you are in covenant with God, your prayer shall prevail; and if you are striving, groaning, and wrestling in prayer, he sees it; and through his grace you shall obtain what you pray for according to his will. Is not this infinite condescension, that he should be near to all that call upon him in truth? We have free liberty through Christ to come with boldness to a throne of grace.

His clemency appears in restoring us after repeated sins. If a prince forgives a rebel, let him take care how he offends again; but God says to his people, "Thou hast played the harlot with many lovers: yet return again to me." He forgives, intending still to forgive more. He forgives iniquity, transgression, and sin. It is not customary among men that there should be a door of mercy open after repeated sins; but in this way it is with God; he will not cast off his people but forgive them again and again. So, he is full of clemency to poor sinners, and proves that he is essentially the God of all grace.

2. He appears as the God of all grace, *in the favors he bestows upon sinners.* That he is the God of all grace in this respect will be evident if we consider the unworthiness of the objects who enjoy this favor. No blessing we receive, whether common or special, is merited by us, "They got not the land in possession by their own sword, neither did their own arm save them: but thy right hand, and thine arm, and the light of thy countenance, because thou hadst a favor unto them," (Psa. 94:3). God first loves persons, from eternity, and then manifests it to them, "The Lord did not set his love upon you, nor choose you, because ye were more in number than any people; for ye were the fewest of all people; but because the Lord loved you," (Deut. 7:7-8). So God bestows his favor on persons, because it is his pleasure to do so. Consider the favor of God in the means and conduit through which it is conveyed to the children of men; that is, Jesus Christ the only mediator between God and man. Had it not been for Christ we never should have had God's favor, nor the happy effects of it. We are by nature the children of wrath, "but now, in Christ Jesus, ye who sometimes were far

off, are made nigh by the blood of Christ," (Eph. 2:13). Until we are reconciled to God by the blood of Christ, we cannot see his face; but Christ has appeased his Father's wrath, and now he says, "This is my beloved Son, in whom I am well pleased," and we are made accepted in the beloved.

Consider the properties of God's love and favor, and he will appear as, "the God of all grace." The favor of God is everlasting; it is from everlasting in the root of it, and to everlasting in its effects, "The mercy of the Lord is from everlasting to everlasting upon them that fear him." As it did not begin in time, so neither will it end in time; as it had no beginning, so neither will it have an end. Christ, "having loved his own which were in the world, he loved them unto the end." Sometimes God's people may lose the sense of his love, but it is always fixed on them, "Who shall separate us from the love of Christ? Shall tribulation, or distress, or persecution, or famine, or nakedness, or peril, or sword? Nay, in all these things we are more than conquerors through him that loved us," (Rom. 8:35, 37). The favor of God is not only everlasting, but it is most free; it must necessarily be free because it is eternal, "I will heal their backsliding, I will love them freely: for mine anger is turned away from him," (Hosea 14:4). This love proceeds from that God who is all sufficient in himself, and needs not any of his creatures to make him happy; it must therefore be free.

Consider the fruits of the divine favor, and it will show that God is, "the God of all grace." The effects of his love are innumerable; for, "eye hath not seen, nor ear heard, neither have entered into the heart of man, the things which God hath prepared for them that love him," (1 Cor. 2:9). All things pertaining to life and godliness are given them by God, whether it respects the life of grace here, or of glory hereafter. "Many, O Lord my God, are thy wonderful works which thou hast done, and thy thoughts which are to usward: they cannot be reckoned up in order unto thee: if I would declare and speak of them, they are more than can be numbered," (Psa. 40:5). We shall now *show,*

II. That God bears an especial favor to his own people above all others. This *appears,*

1. In his great tenderness towards them. Those things that are dear to us we are very tender of; so God is very tender towards his people. In all the afflictions that befall them, he is afflicted with them; their griefs

are grievous to him. His soul is grieved for the miseries of Israel: not so with the wicked, he rejoices over them to destroy them. When Christ ascended into heaven he was out of the reach of all persecutions; but when his people were persecuted he said, "Saul, Saul, why perseeutest thou me? I am Jesus Whom thou persecutest." When a Council was held concerning the apostles, who were called the troublers of the people and such as turned the world upside down, Gamaliel said, *take heed what ye do with these men, for if they are the servants of God ye will be found fighting against him.* "Thus saith the Lord of hosts; he that toucheth you, toucheth the apple of his eye," (Zech. 2:8). Men cannot bear to have their eye touched; so God is as tender of his people as men are of their eyes.

He shows his tenderness over them, by exercising sparing mercies when they have brought themselves into affliction. "He stayeth his south wind in the day of his east wind." He well knows what is proportionable to the strength of his people, and what is necessary for their good; with Ezra, they may say, "Thou, our God, hast punished us less than our iniquities deserve." He will not suffer their afflictions to continue too long, or be too hard on them. Therefore he allays their bitterness; his language is, "I will not contend forever, neither will I be always wroth: for the spirit should fail before me, and the souls which I have made," (Isa. 57:16).

God manifests his tenderness to his people by bearing with their infirmities, "I taught Ephraim also to go, taking them by their arms; but they knew not that I healed them. I drew them with cords of a man, with bands of love," (Hosea 11:3-4). He uses all tenderness to them, as parents to their little children. It was prophesied of Christ, "He shall feed his flock like a shepherd; he shall gather the lambs with his arm, and carry them in his bosom, and shall gently lead those that are with young," (Isa. 40:11). He is willing to do anything for them rather than they should miscarry. Though their graces are imperfect, he will not, "quench, the smoking flame, or break the bruised reed." If there is a sincere love to him in the heart, he will spare them as a man spares his son that loves and serves him, "Like as a father pitieth his children, so the Lord pitieth them that fear him," (Psa. 103:13).

The tenderness of God to his people appeases in that he slights all others for their sakes. He is not so much concerned for whole nations as for a few of his people. "I gave Egypt for thy ransom, Ethiopia and Seba for thee. Since thou wast precious in my sight, thou hast been honourable, and I have loved thee: therefore will I give men for thee, and people for thy life," (Isa. 43:3-4).

His tenderness is also manifested in his readiness to revenge the injuries done them. "I am very sore displeased with the heathen that are at ease: for I was but a little displeased, and they helped forward the affliction," (Zech. 1:15). "When they went from one nation to another, from one kingdom to another people; he suffered no man to do them wrong; yea, he reproved kings for their sakes; saying, touch not mine anointed, and do my prophets no harm," (Psa. 105:13, 15). The people of God are anointed with the spirit of grace and holiness, and those that injure them will find it to be to their own hurt, "Whosoever shall offend one of these little ones that believe in me, it is better for him that a millstone were hanged about his neck, and he were cast into the sea," (Mark 9:42).

2. God manifests his special favor to his people in the gracious promises he has made, to them. These are called, "exceeding great and precious," promises; they are of inestimable, yes, infinite value, and are the

fruits of that eternal love God bears to his people. All his promises are of grace, and spring from that love which God purposed, to manifest to his people. We are by nature so filthy and polluted, that surely nothing in us could move God to take us into his favor, but his own free love and sovereign mercy. "When I passed by thee, and saw thee polluted in thine own blood, I said unto thee when thou wast in thy blood, live," (Ezek. 16:6). Then was the time of love, then I entered into covenant with you, and you became mine. Blessed be, "the God of all grace," for his kind promises of mercy.

3. God manifests his peculiar favor to his people, by the special love tokens he bestows on them. He has given his own Son to die for them; to purchase, by his blood, all the good things of grace and glory that he intends them to enjoy. What a signal effect of love, was this! God did, especially in this, intend the good of his elect. For though our common mercies appear great to us when our hearts are duly impressed with a sense of the divine favor, yet his loving kindness appears much greater in the spiritual blessings which come to us through the death of Christ. Jesus Christ also is the author of all grace in us, "It pleased the Father that in him should all fullness dwell," that, "out of his fullness"

we might receive, "grace, for grace." All the grace that will beautify the soul, either here or hereafter, is given to us through Christ. It is he that works grace in us. There is no grace you can need to make you happy, but it must come from God. He is the fountain from where it flows. He gives his Holy Spirit to them that ask him, and by it he works grace, peace and joy in the hearts of his people. All grace is freely given by God, "If any of you lack wisdom let him ask of God, that giveth to all men liberally and upbraideth not: and it shall be given him," (James 1:5). If you can do nothing in his service, yet you can seek to God for the gift of his Spirit, and, if you do not, this promise will go far to stopping all mouths. If men will seek from God what they need, he will not upbraid them with former sins and provocations, but freely give the blessing sought. In this way God is, "the God of all grace."

CHAPTER 2:
Advantages of Being a True Christian

Secondly, we come to show what advantage it is to a true Christian that he can so look on God as, "the God of all grace."

1. A sense of God, as, "the God of all grace", draws out the soul of a true Christian in love to him. It is a great punishment not to feel love to God, but a great happiness to place our whole delight in him, and to say with Asaph, "Whom have I in heaven but thee? and there is none upon, earth that I desire beside thee." If you have made God your choice as your portion, you may say, "The lines are fallen to me in pleasant places: yea, I have a goodly heritage." Who is a God like our God? He can work in us whatever is good, and he is willing to do it. Everything that is sweet, good, and excellent, is to be found in him and received from him. The consideration that he is, "the God of all grace," will help the Christian to trust in him in all cases and conditions. "Trust in him at all times ye people for they that know thy name will put their trust in thee; for thou, Lord, hast not forsaken them that seek him," (Psa.

9:10). It is an honor God expects from us that we should trust him continually. He will have your confidence placed in him for he is, "the God of all grace." You have great reason to trust in him at all times, for whatever you need he is able to do it. Therefore, set your Christian faith in his almighty power. Whatever you desire, if it will be for your good, you shall have, "No good thing will he withhold from them that walk uprightly." What a firm foundation does this lay for our confidence, to leave all to him who is, "the God of all grace."

3. The consideration of his being, "the God of all grace," encourages the Christian in prayer. What a help it is in prayer to know we are going to, "the God of all grace," and cannot go more often than be greatly welcomed. When we ask him to bless us, and supply our needs, we apply to the inexhaustible fountain of all goodness.

4. This consideration tends to make Christians of a more holy and lively conversation. When they consider that there is power enough in Christ to enable them to mortify their corruptions, it will encourage them to seek grace that they may be more spiritual and heavenly. If you simply thought about God as, "the God

of all grace," you would not live so low, nor be so led astray by your corruptions. Go to the Spirit of God as to a well of living waters.

5. It will serve to make Christians more humble, when they consider God is, "the God of all grace." If God is, "the God of all grace," then it proves that the Christian has no grace in him but what comes from God as the author. This humility of spirit is the proper frame of those whom God will visit. Strive to be as nothing in your own esteem, "for God resisteth the proud, but giveth grace to the humble."

6. This consideration should be of use to make a Christian joyful and thankful in all conditions. A Christian may say, I have a gracious God, with whom I can live, and though I have a naughty heart, God can sanctify it, and I have cause to rejoice in the Lord always. Who has so much cause for thankfulness as the Christian? Consider what God is in himself, and how good he is to you, and learn to be thankful. Therefore, "rejoice in the Lord always, and again I say rejoice."

CHAPTER 3:
Application

We shall, now, thirdly, apply the subject.

Is it so that a true Christian in all his addresses to God, can go to him as, "the God of all grace? *Then,*

1. Think of this until your hearts are affected with it. O! Christian, consider if, *the God of all grace* is your God, and you have an interest in all the excellent things that are in him. The consideration of God as, "the God all grace," should move us to persuade such as our living in sin, and the neglect of God in order to seek him. Those who are in such a condition are invited to come to him who is most lovely. How is it then they stand out against all the loving calls from God by his messengers? They do not consider what a gracious God he is, but look upon him in his greatness, power, wrath, and justice. If I am speaking to such, let me remind you, you sin against that God who maintains you in existence while you transgress his laws. He gives you food and raiment, and yet you rebel against him! He has given you your life, and all your enjoyments; yes, you have nothing but what you have from him; *now the goodness of God should lead you to repentance.* When you

need any mercy from his hands, is it not a wonder you have it, seeing you never ask it at his hands? Yet of his infinite goodness you receive it. God may say of a nation ready to perish with famine, here is a sinful people ready to perish, and it would be a good deed to give them none, for they never ask mercy, and when I give it they are *unthankful*. But, though he might in this way speak because they need it, out of his grace and goodness gives it them, though they sin against him when they have it. Surely such goodness should lead to repentance. Remember this life of sin will not always continue, and will it not be bitterness in the end? He shows himself, "the God of all grace," in the terms of mercy he sent you; in every sermon you hear he entreats you by his messengers to be reconciled to him. He even offers to work in you what he requires in his covenant of grace so that heaven and earth, may be ashamed that men should refuse to return to, "the God of all grace."

CHAPTER 4:
The Christian's God, the God of All Grace

"The God of all grace, who hath called us unto his eternal glory by Christ Jesus, after that ye have suffered awhile, make you perfect, stablish, strengthen, settle you," (1 Peter 5:10).

Having, previously shown that it is the great comfort and advantage of a true Christian, in all his addresses to God, to look on him and go to him as, "the God of all grace, we shall now attend to the **Second Doctrine** contained in the text, *That it is the standing privilege of all true Christians, that God, "hath called them unto his eternal glory by Christ Jesus."*

You that are Christians indeed are by Christ Jesus called from sin, Satan, and the world to grace, holiness, and eternal life. You are called to partake of the divine nature, to delight in God as he delights in himself, to be holy as he is holy, and at last to be happy in enjoying him. Eternal glory shall be enjoyed both by soul and body in the eternal world. Christ has purchased it for you, and will bring you to it. But he can be no Christian, who does not have his heart set on this glory which Christ has prepared for all his people. We shall attend to the doctrine of the text in a few ways.

1. By way of Information. If it is the standing privilege of true Christians that they are called to eternal glory by Christ Jesus, we may learn, 1. What it is which distinguishes them from other men. A carnal man's delight is in natural objects; he delights principally in the pleasures, profits, and honors of the world. But it is the desire of a true Christian to live eternally in glory, and he is seeking, "For glory and honor and immortality, eternal life." The present life is only like a, "vapour, that appeareth for a little time, and then vanisheth away;" but heaven and eternal life are those things a Christian desires to enjoy when he dies.

2. We may learn from here to distinguish churches. That church which is all for outward pomp, worldly glory, and present prosperity, and makes these things the character of a true church, is of Rome and Antichrist.[1] But the true church will aim at the same end Christ aimed at when he taught his disciples that his, "kingdom is not of world." The true church will be for the promotion of grace and holiness, the conversion

---

[1] How many churches in the United States today follow this pattern? I tell you, most do. Ed. Note.

of souls, and making them prepared for, "eternal glory by Christ Jesus."

3. We are informed of the sad condition of unconverted men and women. They are out of Christ, and are out of the way that leads to eternal glory; they take up with the pleasures of the flesh, live in sin, and lose eternal glory. Let me remind you who obey the calls of sin and the motions of your own wicked hearts, that if you go on in this way, you will reap shame and disappointment here, *and eternal destruction hereafter*. The true Christian has grace here and glory hereafter; but your condition will be very awful, after having heard of these glorious things, not to enjoy them. Consider that you lose eternal glory for poor things which perish with your use of them, and it will be an aggravation of your misery to think you have lost heaven for things of no worth. You also part with eternal glory for coarse pleasures which you cannot keep, and if you could even always have them, they would not satisfy your souls. Yet you take up with these unsatisfying pleasures to the neglect of salvation. O! what folly is this! Consider when your outward good things leave you, which you have chosen in preference to eternal glory, you will fall into everlasting misery. If you will not be saved by

Jesus Christ from sin and misery, that you may enjoy glory and happiness, you will be condemned by him to shame and everlasting contempt; you will not only lose heaven, but endure pain in hell and God will execute his wrath and vengeance on you. And for what? All this, for preferring worldly pleasures to eternal glory. O! poor sinners! awake out of your security, repent of sin, flee to Christ, and beg his Holy Spirit, that you may not neglect this great salvation.

4. If true Christians, "are called unto eternal glory by Jesus Christ," then we are informed we should clear up the evidences of our interest in this blessing, "Give all diligence to make your calling and election sure," for if you can clear up your effectual calling, you may be assured of an interest in this eternal glory. That you may the better discern this, examine whether you have ever been made sensible of your wretched condition by nature, and whether you have ever been led to see the evil of sin, and made to know what a sad thing it is to rebel against the Most High! Carnal men make nothing of sin, but an awakened soul feels the evil of it. Have you found yourselves to be universally polluted by sin, and guilty of the worst of sins? The convinced sinner finds that he is inclined to every sin,

and that his thoughts are working the wrong way. When your eyes are open, you will see what filthy creatures sin has made you, how your understanding has been darkened, your will perverted, and your affections disordered. Have you been made sensible of the intolerably and unavoidable wrath of God which is due to you for sin? He is of purer eyes than to behold iniquity, neither can he look on sin without detestation. "The wrath of God is revealed from heaven against all ungodliness and unrighteousness of men," and the poor sinner is persuaded that it is due to him for his transgressions. Have you ever been convinced of your inability to help yourself, either against the guilt or power of sin? A convinced sinner has a fearful impotence in himself, either to satisfy God's justice, bear his wrath, or fulfil the divine law. And if you are effectually called, you have found it like this with you. Examine whether you have sincerely closed with Jesus Christ alone, as he is offered in the gospel. He only can help poor sinners, "For there is none other name under heaven given among men, whereby we must be saved," (Acts 4:12). If you are effectually called, you are taken off all your pleas, brought out of all your holds, and made to see there is no way to the Father but by him.

Here you renounce all your own righteousness and strength, and you come to Christ and depend on him alone. You have taken him for your Lord and King, and given yourselves up to him to be renewed, conducted, and saved by him. Examine also that you walk in Christ, "He that saith he abideth in him, ought himself also to walk, even as he walked," (1 John 2:6). His example must be our pattern and rule. Have you then gained some victory over your former lusts, and are you making no, "provision for the flesh, to fulfil the lusts thereof?"

Those who are effectually called, find sin to be a burden to them. Are you willing to know all your sins, and are they a grief and burden to your soul? How is sin entertained by you? If you are true Christians, though you still sin, yet your heart will be bent against it, you will not allow yourselves in it, and it will not reign in you. When you sin, you will have little ease if you are effectually called. "When I kept silence, my bones waxed old through my roaring all the day long." I delayed to repent, but while I did so I had no quiet, no joy of my life; therefore, "I said, I will confess my transgressions unto the Lord; and thou forgavest the iniquity of my sin," (Psa. 32:3 and 5). So if you are truly godly, commit sin, and carry it without repenting, you will be in a woeful condition. And the longer you remain in this state, the more darkness and distress will you experience and have no ease until you confess your sin. Then you will find God to be graciously pleased, to forgive your sin. If you can sin and be contented, sin and not be troubled, it is a sad sign you are yet in an unconverted state.

Those who are effectually called to eternal glory, have the Spirit of God dwelling in them. For, "if any man have not the Spirit of Christ he is none of his." It is by the Spirit that the work of grace is begun, carried on, and perfected in the heart. Examine, therefore, whether you have the Spirit of God to enlighten you. For, "the natural man receiveth not the things of the Spirit of God," but if you have the Spirit, you understand spiritual things spiritually. You will know them with delight and affection, so as to be transformed into their likeness. If you have the Spirit of God you will be enabled to mortify your sins and corruptions, and be helped against the deeds of the flesh. The Spirit of God is a spirit of prayer, and makes, "intercession for saints, according to the will of God." It is a spirit of adoption also by which the people of God are enabled to cry, "Abba! Father," and by it come to the disposition of a child, to love and honor God as their Father. The Holy Spirit is given to the saints, to seal them to the day of redemption, and comfort their hearts.

These who are effectually called to eternal glory, desire to grow in holiness. True religion is a thriving thing, "I press toward the mark for the prize of the high calling of God in Christ Jesus," (Phil. 3:14). A believer finds it necessary to, "grow in grace," and it is a sign of a hypocrite to sit down contented and not desire more.

That man who is effectually called, will constantly seek to, "make his calling and election sure." If you have been set right, you will desire to have assurance of your future happy and glorious state, and it is dangerous to be content without it. This desire of assurance will cause you to attend on God in the use of all appointed means, and so satisfy you of your right to that, "inheritance which is incorruptible, undefiled, and that fadeth not away." We shall now consider the *doctrine,*

II. By way of Exhortation. Let true Christians, who have a claim to this, "eternal glory by Christ Jesus," walk worthy of it. Let us beware how we carry ourselves, lest we lose any part, or any degree of it. Let this glory continually influence our lives, not to take up with mean things, nor to live like the men of the world. Be exhorted to live up to your privileges, and be zealous for God at the remembrance of that eternal glory to which he has called you by Christ Jesus. We ought to do much for him because he has done much for us, and as he is earnest to make us happy. So we should be earnest to promote his glory, and be grieved when we see him dishonored. Let us be thankfully patient under all our crosses, and walk in God's way through all troubles with cheerfulness; for the glory of our Father's house will make amends for all. "I reckon that the sufferings of this present time are not worthy to be compared with the glory which shall be revealed in us," (Rom. 8:18). Let us learn to be humble and cheerful at all times, and be thankful to God for the hope of "eternal glory." The consideration of this eternal glory, to which he has called us by Christ Jesus, should make us to be of a great mind. We should scorn sin as below us, and resolve to contend with our greatest lusts. It should also be a check to *passion*. To be in a passion for everything is very unbecoming those who hope for eternal glory. Do not let every little business disturb you, but be thankful to God things are no worse with you, and that you have better things in prospect than this world can afford. Learn to forgive all injuries seeing God has forgiven you, and received you into his favor. Let us aim at communion with Jesus Christ in every prayer we offer, and in every sermon we hear, that, "our fellowship be with the Father and with his Son Jesus Christ." Let us be exhorted to live above all the threats and allurements of this world, for they can neither give heaven, nor rob us of it; and let us fear nothing but sin. Let us aim to do all the good we can, and so resemble our Father which is in heaven. This is the glory of our life while in this world. Finally, think frequently of this glory which is prepared for you. If you are true Christians, you are laboring for heaven; therefore frequently visit it in your meditations, and think how happy your state will be when you go to the spirits of the just made perfect,—to your God and Father,—to your Lord and Savior; and let your hearts be lifted up when you think, that when Christ, who is your life shall appear, you, "shall be like him, for you shall see him as he is."

CHAPTER 5:
The Believer's Rest in the God of All Grace

"There remaineth therefore a rest the people of God," (Hebrews 4:9).

The **DOCTRINE** of the text is, that there is a sure, perfect, and everlasting rest prepared for and assigned to the people of God through Jesus Christ the blessed Mediator and only Messiah who is the God of all grace. This is, indeed, *the summary of the whole gospel.* This rest is appropriated to the people of God; those that are in covenant with him and converted to him. It is begun in grace; for as soon as men are brought into a state of grace they enter into peace. Grace is glory begun, and glory is grace perfected. I shall endeavor to set out the doctrine, in allusion to that rest the Israelites had in the wilderness,—in Canaan,—on the Sabbath.

I. The Israelites had rest in the wilderness. In the wilderness they had rest from that bondage they experienced in Egypt: so the people of God are brought over to Christ, and find rest in him, even in this life. A state of grace is a state of rest, in comparison with a state of nature; for when men take Christ's yoke upon them, they find that special rest and peace which they will not exchange for all the pleasures of sin. In the wilderness the Israelites had Moses for their leader, who was a holy, wise, and gracious man. So the people of God in this wilderness world have a blessed leader, the Lord Jesus Christ. For, though he is in glory, he leads them by his Spirit. In the wilderness they had the tabernacle of witness, the sacrifices and worship of God; so we in this world have the precious ordinances to wait on God. They had angel's food in the wilderness, manna fell daily round about their tents. Here we have the dew of heaven, the power and influences of the Holy Spirit to live on. There is this difference, our manna falls especially on the Sabbath day, theirs did not. They were wonderfully supplied and provided for as they traveled through the wilderness. So we, though we have many needs while here, yet God supplies them all by Christ Jesus. We have a God to go to at all times. They had help against the many evils which befell them during their passage through the wilderness. When they were stung by fiery serpents, they had a brazen serpent to which they might look and live. So we, when stung by sin, have Christ to look to, and as the serpent was lifted up, so Christ in the gospel is exalted and we find healing in him. They were often beset with trials in the wilderness, but God always delivered them and they came off conquerors. So we are assaulted on every side by Satan, the world and the flesh, yet we are delivered by Christ, and in him we are more than conquerors.

II. The Israelites' great rest was in Canaan. 1. They were there settled in a land provided for them. They came to, "goodly cities which they builded not, and houses full of all good things, which they, filled not, and wells digged which they digged not, vineyards and olive trees which they planted not." So our chief rest is in heaven, and when we come there we shall find everything already provided for us – a mansion prepared by Christ, and a city which has foundations whose builder and maker is God.

2. When they came to Canaan all their failings, tossings, and uncertainties ceased. Their sins made it a forty year journey to arrive in Canaan. They were sometimes near it but for their transgressions were sent back again. So we, while in this world, sometimes think we are pretty near heaven, and make ourselves sure of

it. But we sin and are driven back again to sojourn a little longer. When we arrive at heaven, all anxieties and uncertainties will cease, and we shall sit down with Abraham, and Isaac, and Jacob, in the kingdom of God. Here we lose sight of heaven many times; but in heaven we shall enter into our rest and go out no more forever.

3. In Canaan the Jews had no further occasion to murmur; they entered upon the enjoyment of the many good things promised; so when we enter into heaven we shall murmur no more, nor find fault with our condition any more: for everything will be to our mind.

4. In Canaan the Israelites obtained a supply for all their needs; hunger, and thirst, and clothes were all taken away. So when we once enter our heavenly Canaan, all our needs will be supplied, or rather prevented, "They shall hunger no more, neither thirst anymore; neither shall the sun light on them, nor any heat. For the lamb which is in the midst of the throne shall feed them, and shall lead them unto living fountains of waters; and God shall wipe away all tears from their eyes," (Rev. 7:16-17).

5. In the wilderness the Jews had the tabernacle of witness and altars; but in Canaan they had a magnificent temple. So we, while here, have precious ordinances in which, we enjoy communion with God; but in heaven we shall have a glorious temple, "I saw no temple therein: for the Lord God Almighty and the Lamb are the temple of it," (Rev. 21:22).

III. The Israelites had their Sabbath's and there remains the keeping of a Sabbath for the people of God. There is a resemblance between a Sabbath and heaven in several particulars.

1. On the Sabbath, we have rest by authority from bodily labors. God has made it unlawful to work, and sweat, and toil on the Sabbath; so when we come to heaven we shall rest from all labor. We will be done with earthly working; but our works shall follow, and we enjoy the comfort though not suffer their toil. It is said, "In six days the Lord made heaven and earth, the sea, and all that in them is, and rested the seventh day," that is, he was refreshed, he looked on all he had done, and was mightily pleased, for all was very good; so the believer shall rest in heaven, and have comfort in all the toil that is past.

2. On the Sabbath day there is, or ought to be, a rest from sin. So David resolved, "I will wash my bands in innocency: so will I compass thine altar, O Lord." There can be no coming to God in pollution, no acceptable worshiping of him in sin; so in heaven there will be no sin, for without holiness, "no man shall see the Lord."

3. On the Sabbath day common things are laid aside. It is sinful to meddle with our common affairs on the Lord's day; so when we come to heaven, we shall leave all worldly and common things behind, never more to return to them.

4. On that Sabbath, spiritual worship is offered to God, in which gracious souls delight much in. On this holy day they have opportunity to render their service to Almighty God. The great employment of the Sabbath is praising and admiring God, for the creation and redemption of the world by Jesus Christ. And it is a good thing to give thanks to the Lord, and to sing, "praises to thy name, O! Most High," (Psa. 92:1). The more we are carried out in the work of the Sabbath, the better we keep the day, and the sweeter it is to us. In heaven the work of praising and blessing God will continue, forevermore.

5. The Sabbath is a day of instruction, "One thing have I desired of the Lord, that will I seek after; that I may dwell in the house of the Lord all the days of my life, to behold the beauty of the Lord, and to inquire in his temple," (Psa. 27:4). The Psalmist desired that he might see God and be taught by him; and gracious souls usually have some new discovery made to them on the Sabbath, and so increase in knowledge. So heaven is a place of instruction, for there you will understand in a moment, what you cannot attain to here with all your pain and labor.

6. On the Sabbath, holy impressions, and divine transformations, often take place on the souls of men. People come one way to the ordinance of the house of God, and go away a very different way, they are cast into another mold; profane and unclean people become pious and holy, and drooping souls are filled with joy. So when we enter heaven, we shall be transformed to this purpose; sin will be banished away, and all trouble will take its leave; never to return.

7. The Sabbath is made more comfortable by good company. It does a gracious soul good to see God and Jesus Christ worshipped in such a state. When there is a great blessing on holy assemblies, nothing is

so like heaven. There is much of God when his precious servants join heartily together in the praises of God. But in heaven, what a flame of joy will there be in the hearts of God's people when they all join in loving and adoring their blessed Creator and Redeemer for evermore!

8. Saints on the Sabbath have communion with God, and satisfaction in his house. They are, "abundantly satisfied with the fatness of his house." If there is anything like satisfaction on earth, it is to be found in the house of God on the Sabbath day. David thought so, when in the wilderness of Judah he thirsted to see the power and glory of God, so as he had seen him in the sanctuary, "Thus I will bless thee while I live," he said, "I will lift up my hands in thy name," (Psa. 43:4). God's loving kindness is better than all the comforts of life. In heaven saints have full satisfaction, "In thy presence is fullness of joy; at thy right hand there are pleasures for evermore." "I shall be satisfied, when I awake, with thy likeness." The believing soul may say, when I spring into eternity, or arise from the dead, I shall see you as you are, be made like to you, and be so filled with joy that there shall be no room for any more. Now if Sabbath days on earth are so sweet, on

account of the various things we have mentioned, what will be that Sabbath we shall keep with God in heaven! Then, we shall sin no more, and meddle with common things no more. But be wholly taken up in praising God, and living in the embraces of God forever. Surely an eternal Sabbath is happiness enough; and this rest remains for the people of God. They shall go up into the mount, and there enjoy sweet and satisfying communion with God, and come down no more.

We shall now show the *improvement* to be made of this subject.

It should teach us to improve our present Sabbaths, that they may be helps to fit and prepare us for heaven, that eternal Sabbath which remains for the people of God. It may also serve to comfort the believer under the afflictions he may meet with in the world; as, the malignity of men, the shaking of nations, the divisions of the church, the inward doubts and troubles he endures, and the uncertainty of his present condition in the world. Perhaps when delivered from one affliction we are soon in another, and we find we have no rest here; but this may comfort us, there remains a rest for the people of God. A time is coming when we shall never be exercised with crosses anymore. Suppose that your condition in life is pleasant to you, and circumstances are such as afford you comfort; if you belong to the people of God, all the good you enjoy here is but a taste of what you shall enjoy in heaven, where all shall be perfected and ratified. If the people of God are laboring under such weakness of body that they cannot go up to his house, and enjoy the benefit of public ordinances; yet this should comfort them, there is a period coming when they shall keep an eternal Sabbath with the general assembly in heaven, and shall dwell in the house of the Lord forever with the God of all grace. In case we have lost any dear and pious relatives, let us not sit weeping over their graves, but up and be doing; let us travel on and make haste after them to that rest into which they have entered; and which remains for all the people of God.

APPENDIX:
The House of God Remembered in Sickness

"What is the sign that I shall go up to the house of the Lord?" (Isaiah 38:22).

When the Holy Spirit had spoken of this of king Hezekiah in the book of the Kings, he spoke largely of him. In this chapter of Isaiah we have a particular account of his sickness, his prayer, and his recovery. Observe, he does not say what shall be the sign that I shall live again? But, "what is the sign that I shall go up to the house of the Lord?"

The **DOCTRINE** is this, *That the chief thing of which a good man accounts in his recovery from sickness, is, that he may, "go up to the house of the Lord," and give thanks to God for his recovery.*

David resolved that he would declare the goodness of the Lord in the great congregation, "Why art thou cast down, O my soul? and why art thou disquieted within me? hope thou in God: for I shall yet praise him, who is the health of my countenance, and my God?" (Psa. 42:11). *I shall,*

I. Briefly consider, what this going up to the house of the Lord is. The psalmist's principal desire was, that he might, "dwell in the house of the Lord all the days of his life, to behold the beauty of the Lord, and to inquire in his temple," (Psa. 27:4). We read of some who did not depart from the house of the Lord, but were always there when anything was to be done, so they might not miss the morning duty, nor evening sacrifice. It is our duty also to wait on God's house when anything is going on there. But I shall, II. Show you why a good man ought to fix on his going to the house of God, on his recovery from sickness.

1. From the remembrance that good men have of the house of God in their sickness. If we rightly understand things, we shall think well of the ordinances of God's house. They are precious things in our lifetime, and they will appear so when sickness and death draw near. Religion is the best thing that can be. A good man in sickness is convinced of his neglect in going to the house of God when he was in health and had opportunity; and longs to be restored that he may go and obtain something for aftertime.

2. God is more immediately and principally served in his house. God should be served in our

callings, but he is more especially honored in the assemblies of the saints, "Blessed are they that dwell in thy house, they will be still praising thee," (Psa. 84:4).

3. The work of God's home ties together the whole of a Christian's work. The whole of a Christian's life may be considered as having reference to the Sabbath day; for it has an influence upon the whole of our business. The whole employment of a Christian is but a right preparation for going to the house of the Lord, "I will wash mine hands in innocency. So will I compass thine altar, O Lord," (Psa. 26:6). If men in the midst of the week thought of going to the house of the Lord, O! how it would influence them to avoid many evils and quicken them in holy duties.

4. In the house of God spiritual provision is obtained for the support and nourishment of their soul. The Sabbath is the market and fair day for the soul. A Christian's care lies about the matter of God's ordinances. For, the business of the soul should be most looked after. There is small hope of getting our hearts up in our callings when they are down at God's ordinances. When we go up to the house of the Lord, we have opportunities of receiving spiritual blessings;

and whatever we need in our spiritual course may be found here.

5. Another reason why a good man wishes to recover from sickness that he may go up to the house of the Lord, is, because there the greatest joy and comfort are experienced. It is the next to heaven of any place in this world, "How amiable are thy tabernacles, O Lord of hosts!" The very walls are lovely, yes, everything is lovely when God is there.

If it is inquired, why it was not Hezekiah's desire to die, as well as to live? I may reply, because things may so happen that it may be a great mercy for such to live in regard of others. How does this reprove those who have been restored from sickness, but keep away from, "the house of the Lord?"

Our subject, 1. Informs us, that, good men should pray, if it may be, that as long as they live, they may not be long detained from the house of God, David, "the king said unto Zaddok, carry back the ark of God into the city; if I shall find favor in the eyes of the Lord, he will bring me again, and show me both it and his habitation," (2 Sam. 15:25). It is the business of health to wait on the Lord in his house; for when we are sick we cannot go there. Yet there is this consolation, that wherever the Lord has his children, there will his presence be. Hagar, "called the name of the Lord that spake unto her, 'Thou God seest me,'" (Gen. 16:13).

2. We may learn the sad condition of a wicked sick man—one that is unacquainted with the, "house of the Lord, and the still worse state of those that have been sick, but never were sorry for their absence from the house of God. "Blessed is the man whose strength is in thee, whose heart are the ways of them. Who passing through the valley of Baca make it a well," (Psa. 84:5-6). Every man's heart runs one way or another and the child of God's way is toward the house of the Lord.

3. We are informed that it is a great mercy under afflictions, whom people have a desire to go up to the house of the Lord, and when their sickness is not so great as to prevent them. Let any of us that have been sick endeavor especially to improve going up to the house of God. By the sickness among us, God perhaps aims at that coldness in his ordinances and the little account we make of meeting him in his house. May we learn to value them more. *Amen.*

www.ingramcontent.com/pod-product-compliance
Lightning Source LLC
Chambersburg PA
CBHW021915040426
42447CB00007B/862